TOP SECRET SCIENCE IN

CYBERCRIME AND ESPIONAGE

Ellen Rodger

CRABTREE
PUBLISHING COMPANY
WWW.CRABTREEBOOKS.COM

TOP SECRET SCIENCE

Author: Ellen Rodger

Editors: Sarah Eason, Honor Head, Harriet McGregor, and Janine Deschenes

Proofreaders: Sally Scrivener, Tracey Kelly, and Wendy Scavuzzo

Editorial director: Kathy Middleton

Design: Lynne Lennon

Cover design: Paul Myerscough and Jeni Child

Photo research: Rachel Blount

Production coordinator and prepress technician: Ken Wright

Print coordinator: Katherine Berti

Consultant: David Hawksett

Produced for Crabtree Publishing by Calcium Creative

Photo Credits:

t=Top, tr=Top Right, tl=Top Left

Inside: FBI: p. 15t; Shutterstock: Africa Studio: p. 6; Carlos Amarillo: pp. 30–31t; BeeBright: pp. 27, 44; Tony Craddock: p. 41b; Rob Crandall: p. 19; Danielo: p. 5t; Dfree: pp. 20–21; Drop of Light: p. 18; Ekaterina Minaeva: p. 17t; Richard Frazier: p. 23; Gorodenkoff: pp. 4–5t; iDEAR Replay: p. 45; Sergey Kohl: pp. 3, 43; Wong yu Liang: pp. 10–11b; TY Lim: p. 13b; Blazej Lyjak: p. 25; M-SUR: p. 38; Sharaf Maksumov: p. 33t; MatiasDelCarmine: pp. 12–13t; MikeDotta: pp. 1, 29; Volodymyr Nikitenko: p. 9; Palidachan: pp. 14–15t; Rawpixel.com: pp. 8, 31br, 36; Ricochet64: p. 34; Prachaya Roekdeethaweesab: p. 42; Bart Sadowski: pp. 40–41t; Rena Schild: p. 39; Sdecoret: p. 7; Joe Seer: pp. 24, 35; Joseph Sohm: p. 22; SpeedKingz: p. 11t; Andrey Suslov: p. 21r; Vadven: pp. 32–33; Wachiwit: p. 28; Bing Wen: p. 37; Vladimir Wrangel: p. 26; U. S. Army: U. S. Army photo by Steve Stover: pp. 16–17b.

Cover: Shutterstock: Gorodenkoff.

Library and Archives Canada Cataloguing in Publication

Rodger, Ellen, author
    Top secret science in cybercrime and espionage / Ellen Rodger.

(Top secret science)
Includes index.
Issued in print and electronic formats.
ISBN 978-0-7787-5992-8 (hardcover).--
ISBN 978-0-7787-5998-0 (softcover).--
ISBN 978-1-4271-2241-4 (HTML)

    1. Computer crimes--Juvenile literature. 2. Internet in espionage-
-Juvenile literature. 3. Espionage--Juvenile literature. 4. Electronics
in espionage--Juvenile literature. 5. Electronic surveillance--Juvenile
literature. 6. Computer security--Juvenile literature. I. Title. II. Title:
Cybercrime and espionage.

HV6773.R634 2019   j327.120285'4678   C2018-905656-8
                                                                              C2018-905657-6

Library of Congress Cataloging-in-Publication Data

Names: Rodger, Ellen, author.
Title: Top secret science in cybercrime and espionage / Ellen Rodger.
Description: New York, New York : Crabtree Publishing, [2019] |
    Series: Top secret science | Audience: Ages 10-14. |
    Audience: Grades 7 to 8. | Includes index.
Identifiers: LCCN 2018053383 (print) | LCCN 2018054835 (ebook) |
    ISBN 9781427122414 (Electronic) |
    ISBN 9780778759928 (hardcover : alk. paper) |
    ISBN 9780778759980 (pbk. : alk. paper)
Subjects: LCSH: Computer crimes--Juvenile literature. | Computer
    crimes--Prevention--Juvenile literature. | Internet in espionage--
    Juvenile literature. | Information technology--Juvenile literature.
Classification: LCC HV8079.C65 (ebook) |
    LCC HV8079.C65 R63 2019 (print) | DDC 364.16/8--dc23
LC record available at https://lccn.loc.gov/2018053383

Crabtree Publishing Company

www.crabtreebooks.com   1-800-387-7650

Printed in the U.S.A./042019/CG20190215

Published in Canada
Crabtree Publishing
616 Welland Ave.
St. Catharines, ON
L2M 5V6

Published in the United States
Crabtree Publishing
PMB 59051
350 Fifth Avenue, 59th Floor
New York, NY 10118

Published in the United Kingdom
Crabtree Publishing
Maritime House
Basin Road North, Hove
BN41 1WR

Published in Australia
Crabtree Publishing
Unit 3 – 5 Currumbin Court
Capalaba
QLD 4157

CONTENTS

CHAPTER 1

THE DARK FUTURE

Robbing a bank used to mean people with guns breaking into a building and taking money. Today, people living thousands of miles away can carry out **cyberattacks** on banks. Cyberattacks are committed when people attack computer systems and **networks** using **coding** and computers as weapons. This type of crime is relatively new. It did not exist before modern computers and has greatly increased since the early 1990s, when the Internet became commonly used by billions of people.

Cybercriminals can operate from anywhere in the world.

CYBERCRIME AS HIGH TECH

According to the International Criminal Police Organization (**Interpol**), cybercrime is a fast-growing field of crime. Cybercrime is any crime in which computer and digital technology are used to commit a crime or are targeted in a crime. Almost any crime that can be committed in the non-cyberworld can also be organized in the cyberworld. These include arranging murders, stealing someone's **identity**, spreading hate or **terrorism**, or **laundering money**. Cybercrime costs the economy billions of dollars. It harms everyone from children and families to governments and major companies. Cyber **espionage** uses computers to **spy**, or get information, about foreign governments. This activity is known as cyberspying.

CATCHING CYBERCRIMINALS

In the United States, the FBI is the lead agency for investigating cybercrime. It works with police agencies within the United States and internationally, such as Interpol. But other police and government agencies investigate these crimes, too. In Canada, the Royal Canadian Mounted Police (RCMP) work with other agencies to fight cybercrime.

DARK SCIENCE SECRETS

Imagine someone receives a Facebook message from a friend to check out a YouTube video. The message contains a "bit.ly" or "t.cn" link and their first name. Safe to click on, right? That is what thousands of people thought in 2017 when they fell victim to a **malware** attack intended to get their personal data. When the victims clicked the link, the malware redirected them to a set of websites that took information about their computer browser and operating system. Cybersecurity experts, Kaspersky Lab, say the people behind the attack were probably making money from ads and getting access to Facebook accounts.

CYBERCRIME EVOLUTION

There is an old and famous phrase that says "knowledge is power." It means that those who have knowledge can influence people and events. In the cyberworld, information is power. The more data, or information, a cybercriminal has, the more powerful he or she is.

EVOLUTION OF CYBERCRIME

Early cybercrimes were simple letter scams that were sent by e-mail. Criminals sent e-mails claiming they were wealthy princes who needed help accessing their riches. The "princes" convinced recipients to send a small amount of money to them, which would help them access their money. In return, they promised they would send the recipient a share of their millions. Of course, as soon as the recipients sent the money, the "princes" disappeared online.

Cybercriminals can use computers, phones, and their own knowledge of programming and scamming, to pull off crimes.

SMARTER CRIMES

Things were different before the Internet. People shopped in stores or used paper catalogs to buy through the mail. Newspapers and magazines published only on paper because there was no social media. Cybercrime was largely directed at businesses and government computer networks. The **hackers** wanted to prove their skills and, if possible, make some money.

The Internet makes everything more convenient. It also makes it easier for criminals in distant parts of the world to commit cybercrimes.

NETWORKING CRIMES

Today, the Internet is a global computer network that provides information and tools to connect computers. It allows people to communicate, do business, shop, bank, and have fun. It is also a playground for hackers and cybercriminals. However, the very first **virus** was made even before the Internet existed—in 1971. A virus is computer **software** designed to cause damage. Called Creeper, it infected corporate computers, but it did not cause damage.

DARK SCIENCE SECRETS

At age 16, Kevin Mitnick hacked his first computer network. That was in 1979, back before the Internet. Mitnick gained unauthorized access to the network computer company Digital Equipment Corporation, where he copied software. He was charged, convicted, and spent time in jail. Upon his release, he continued to hack and went on the run for several years while the FBI was looking for him. Mitnick was eventually caught and spent five years in prison for computer **fraud**. When he got out, he wrote books on hacking and became a computer **security consultant** for companies that wanted to protect their data against hackers. He used his knowledge to become a cybersecurity expert.

EVER-EVOLVING CRIMES

It is tough to keep on top of the new and inventive ways cybercriminals think up to steal money, shut down systems, and cause havoc. Cybercrime is ever-evolving and criminals are always thinking one step ahead.

Transferring

75 %

PHIS

Stealing data can be as simple as tricking people into giving out their passwords.

SMART CRIMINALS

In addition to scams, cybercriminals now hack into computer systems and networks to steal data. Some cybercriminals attack computer networks with viruses to destroy for the sake of destroying, or hold networks for "ransom." The list of rip-offs, spoofs, and attacks now done through the cyberworld is almost endless. Cybercriminals have become much more creative and sophisticated in their attempts to get information from unsuspecting people. But the goal is the same—to con and fool people into giving them their personal information. These types of crimes are called phishing expeditions, because the cybercriminal tries to "lure" victims with offers such as free gifts.

DARK SCIENCE SECRETS

Today, viruses are major threats to computer security. They are a type of malware, which is short for **malicious** software—any software that is meant to damage a computer. Viruses can be combatted by antivirus software, but new viruses are constantly being developed. The damage caused by viruses is costly. The MyDoom worm virus, developed in 2003–04, caused $35 billion in damages to business and home computers. Worm viruses **replicate**, or copy, themselves and spread to other computers. MyDoom spread through e-mail. It caused people to not be able to send or receive e-mails from their Microsoft-based accounts. To this date, nobody knows who programmed the virus.

SINISTER CYBERCRIME

The tentacles of cybercrime have a far reach—affecting big corporations as well as ordinary people on their home computers throughout the world. Cybercrime has life-altering, and sometimes life-ending consequences for victims. According to the Norton Cybercrime Report, 65 percent of the adults it polled had been a victim of some kind of cybercrime.

NAMELESS AND FACELESS

Many of the people interviewed for the Norton Report said they did not expect cybercriminals to be "brought to justice" because they were unknown or living in countries far away from where they committed crimes. Many blamed themselves for becoming victims, because some cybercrime involves gaining the victim's trust. This is particularly true for people who fall for **confidence schemes** or **sweetheart scams** in which the scammer fools the victim into thinking they are in a relationship.

Victims may blame themselves for the crimes committed by cybercriminals. They think they must have done something to be targeted.

DARK SCIENCE SECRETS

Amanda Todd was 15 years old when she committed suicide in 2012, after being bullied and harassed online. Amanda had been blackmailed by a **cyberstalker** into showing naked images of herself. Her stalker used the images to harass her. When she moved or switched schools to escape, Amanda's cyberstalker would find her and send her new school friends the images. After Amanda's death, police identified her cyberstalker. He was sentenced to 10 years in jail.

CYBER LOVE SCAMS

People who are taken in by sweetheart scams are not stupid. They are often lonely or trusting, which is what the cyberscammers count on. A wealthy Hong Kong businesswoman was conned out of $23 million dollars by a British man armed with a computer and sweet words. In 2014, the man befriended the woman on an online dating site. He cheated her out of her money over the course of four years by convincing her that he needed business loans. She transferred money to bank accounts throughout Asia and Europe without ever meeting him. Online sweetheart scams like this earn cybercriminals billions of dollars a year.

Cyberbullying takes place over cell phones, computers, or tablets. Sometimes victims know their bullies. Other times, they are complete strangers.

HACK ATTACK

Hackers who work for good are called white hats. Black hats are malicious hackers who want to do harm. Gray hats are hackers that can go either way.

Hackers have been around for almost as long as there have been computers. They are **programmers** who can hack computers and networks. Some hackers steal information that could harm governments, businesses, and people. Others seek to make money. Other hackers enjoy the thrill or challenge of hacking—but do not threaten people or businesses. Some of these hackers even go so far as to insist the term hacker only means people who use their computer skills for good.

HACKER GROUPS

In the early days of personal computers, hacker groups were unofficial circles of computer experts who broke into computer systems and shared information. Their computer expertise and skills gave them the edge. In the 1980s, there were few laws against hacking because personal computers and the crimes committed with them were new. Today, hackers can be charged with a number of crimes—if they can be identified and caught, which is often difficult. Many hackers are in it for the thrill of competition—beating other hackers or shutting down a computer network. Some enjoy the excitement of making money by ripping off businesses and banks. Others are paid by their governments to hack.

BEARS AND KITTENS

Energetic Bear and Magic Kitten are the names of two of the most dangerous hacker groups. Some are **sponsored**, or paid, by governments to hack into key computer systems in another country. These groups are called state hackers. China's state hackers use the keyword "Panda," such as Deep Panda, Hurricane Panda, and Putter Panda, in their hacking campaigns. In 2014, five Putter Panda hackers were charged by the U.S. Department of Justice for stealing **trade secrets** from American **nuclear** and solar technology companies.

DARK SCIENCE SECRETS

Park Jin Hyok is a busy hacker. He is said to work as a cyber **operative** for the North Korean government. He is accused of being part of a team that among other crimes, stole $81 million from Bangladesh Bank in 2016, launched the WannaCry **ransomware** in 2017, and broke into Sony Pictures in 2014. The FBI charged Park with computer-related fraud in September 2018 when he was just 23 years old. However, he is thought to live in North Korea and there is no way to bring him to the United States to face the charges.

The WannaCry malware affected more than 200,000 computers in 150 countries.

WannaCry ransomware
You are at risk

THE CYBERCRIMINAL NEXT DOOR

What makes a cybercriminal do what they do? It seems the motivations are not always about money. Sometimes it is for the laughs (LOLZ), and sometimes it is to prove the hacker's hacking abilities to his or her peers. Many cybercrimes can seem "victimless," which is why some cybercriminals convince themselves they are doing no harm by hacking.

HACKER-FOR-HIRE

Karim Baratov was 12 years old when he taught himself to code, then later to hack. At age 15, he claimed to have made his first $1 million. By the time he was 22, he was a multimillionaire with his own house and expensive cars. But his success and freedom did not last. By the time he was 23, the Canadian hacker-for-hire was serving five years in a U.S. jail for hacking and **economic** espionage. Baratov had taken part in a 2014 hack of Yahoo, sponsored by the Russian government. The **breach** stole data from 500 million users. Baratov used the data to gain access to the e-mail accounts of Russian journalists, and business and government officials. Baratov's lawyers said he did not know he was working for Russian spies.

If cybercriminals are identified and caught they may need to pay a fine, or they may spend time in jail.

MOST WANTED

FBI "most wanted" lists are nothing new. The crime lists show headshots of wanted criminals and have been posted on the walls of post offices and police stations for decades. Some people on the recent "most wanted" cybercrime list are foreign hackers whose crimes include hacking into **e-mail service providers** to steal confidential information, and organizing fraud rings that sell fake software by taking over browsers and putting up false messages. A lot of cybercrime is **gang crime**, in which hackers work together as a group.

w.fbi.gov/wanted/cyber

> MOST WANTED

MOST WANTED

Ten Most Wanted | Fugitives | Terrorism | Kidnappings/Miss
Crimes Against Children | Murder | Additional Violent Crimes

Cyber's Most Wanted
Select the images of suspects to display more information.

Search for [Search for...]

Results: 63 Items

The FBI has a most wanted webpage dedicated to cybercriminals. It posts pictures of the criminals and describes their cybercrimes.

TOMORROW'S SECRETS

Some governments and companies pay hackers money called **"bug** bounties" to find faults in their systems. Developers then fix the bugs, or problems with the software, and prevent malicious hacking. Microsoft and Facebook sponsored a program named the Internet Bug Bounty to improve Internet security. Around $700,000 was paid out to "friendly hackers" who hacked Internet software and exposed its weaknesses. This type of high expenditure on fighting hacking may increase in the future as cybercrime becomes an even greater threat.

HACKER GROUPS

Hacker networks are groups of hackers who work together on large projects, efforts, or scams. They do not work together in the same building (that we know of), but instead link through online networks. When black hat hackers work together, they can do a lot of damage. Similarly, white hat hackers working together can do a lot of good.

CREWS, GANGS, AND COLLECTIVES

Many hacker groups have names such as TeaMp0isoN, Level Seven Crew, or Global Hell. In 1999, black hat hackers Level Seven became famous for trashing the website of the U.S. Embassy in China. The group replaced the homepage with racist and anti-government statements. The group was thought to have made 60 **incursions** of computer systems in 1999, sometimes for money but often to make a point.

Global Hell was a black hat group that acted like a street gang. Its leaders were teenagers when they hacked into the White House website and **defaced** it, or spoiled its appearance. Another member defaced the U.S. army website. Group members were tracked down and sent to jail, and the gang fell apart in the early 2000s.

The U.S. army has a cybercrime division that tracks criminals all over the world.

Black hat hacker groups often steal and deal in stolen credit card numbers.

HUMAN RIGHTS AND FREEDOM

Chaos Computer Club (CCC) is the largest hacker group in Europe. It hacked into a German bank to steal money—only to return it a day later. The hacker group claims it is "white hat," and regularly defends **digital rights**. Most of CCC's actions are on the side of human rights and freedom. It urges the German government not to launch cyberattacks on people or governments. CCC holds events for hackers, publishes a magazine, and posts their activities online.

DARK SCIENCE SECRETS

ShadowCrew was a major cybercrime gang that dealt in stolen identification, credit cards, and bank cards. It was shut down in 2004. ShadowCrew members were business students and **mortgage brokers**, or people who arrange mortgages to buy property. They used phishing to get credit card details, then used them to buy goods. The goods were then sold online. The gang raked in more than $4 million before it was shut down. Crew members were charged with fraud-related crimes, tried, and sent to jail.

STATE-SANCTIONED HACKERS

State-sponsored cyberattacks are the new threat to international peace and security. Cyberspace is the battlefield. In March 2018, at the World Economic Forum in Davos, Switzerland, many world leaders revealed that they fear cyberattacks more than terrorism, disease, or even nuclear weapons.

The World Economic Forum is an organization that holds annual meetings for business, education, and political leaders. They discuss important world issues.

CYBER SABOTAGE

In 2015, 230,000 people in Ukraine were the victims of a cyberattack that cut power to homes and businesses. It was the first known cyberattack of a **power grid**, or network for delivering electricity. Foreign state hackers show their power by attacking the computers that run power grids and other public utilities. In 2018, the U.S. government said that Russian cyber agents had targeted power plants, water processing plants, and air transportation facilities in the United States. Energy Secretary Rick Perry said cyberattacks are "happening hundreds of thousands of times a day."

Annual Meeting 2018

WORLD ECONOMIC FORUM
COMMITTEE IMPROVING OF TH

CHINA'S HACKER ARMY

China's hacker army is a state-sanctioned group of hackers. It contains between 50,000 and 100,000 people. Some work for the government, or are part of a military cyber unit called PLA Unit 61398. Others are **civilians**, or people not involved in a military or police force, who work on government cyber espionage projects. In 2014, the U.S. Department of Justice charged five PLA Unit 61398 officers with stealing **intellectual property** from U.S. businesses. Intellectual property is things that people have written or created, including inventions and designs. The hackers steal the ideas to make products and then sell them. PLA Unit 61398 officers stole the intellectual property by planting malware on computers.

DARK SCIENCE SECRETS

Could a group of hackers and social media experts steal people's identities, pose as political activists, and possibly influence the results of an election? The U.S. Department of Justice thinks that they could. In 2018, 13 Russian hackers and three companies were charged with meddling in the 2016 presidential election and carrying out a massive fraud. The hackers manipulated American readers of social media. Their teams created social media accounts that gained hundreds of thousands of followers. They posted false stories about immigration, religion, and race issues. Twitter had more than 3,800 fake Russian accounts that posted 176,000 tweets and videos in the run-up to the election.

Around 126 million Facebook users saw fake Russian-made content about the presidential election. It is believed that this influenced how people voted.

CHAPTER 3

CONNECTED AND VULNERABLE

Our modern world depends on computers and networks to do everything from schedule surgeries in hospitals, assess and pay taxes, and even preserve family photos for future generations. How do you keep your computer and information safe when smart cybercriminals have so many tricks to get what they want?

HACKER DAD

Ryan Collins is a father from Pennsylvania who spent his spare time hacking into the computers of celebrities. He ran a two-year phishing scam in which he took the iCloud and Gmail account passwords of more than 100 people, including actor Jennifer Lawrence and singer Rihanna. Collins sent his targets fake e-mails from Google and Apple to trick them. Once he had their passwords, he stole information and photos from their computer backups. He posted hundreds of images online to photo sharing sites. Collins was tracked down and was sentenced in 2016 to 18 months in jail.

Jennifer Lawrence has said that the hacking of her private photos was a violation that should carry harsher sentences.

CYBER MARKETS

There are many places where cybercriminals sell stolen information and their services as hackers-for-hire. According to the magazine *Business Insider*, some hackers make as much as $80,000 per month, and gangs can make more. In **online forums**, they sell their services, information, images, or malware they have designed. They even sell "exploit kits" or toolkits. These kits provide everything needed to rip people off. They can be used by hackers who do not have coding skills.

14:30 PM

TOMORROW'S SECRETS

Sometimes, all of the connected devices in an IoT network in a household use the same password, making them easy to hack.

The Internet of Things (IoT) is a network of devices that includes home appliances, smart garage door openers, wireless routers, and **video streaming devices**. According to the FBI, cybercriminals search for these devices because they communicate with the Internet. Many do not have good security and use passwords that are easy to hack. These networks are now targets of cybercriminals. Cybercriminals hack IoT devices and use them to send e-mail spam, buy and sell illegal images, and set up scams.

SMART HOME

NOBODY'S SAFE

John Podesta is a smart and powerful man. He served as White House Chief of Staff for one American president and was an adviser to another. But like everyone else with an Internet connection, he was vulnerable to smart cybercriminals.

HACKING A POLITICAL PARTY

In March 2016, Podesta was working as the chairman of Hillary Clinton's campaign for president. He was sent a phishing e-mail to his Google e-mail (Gmail) account. It was a fake message that someone had tried to access his account. Podesta passed the e-mail on to someone else for help. That person mistyped a response. Instead of saying "this is an illegitimate e-mail," they typed "this is a legitimate e-mail." Thinking it was safe, Podesta followed the fake alert's instructions to change his password. This simple act allowed Russian state hackers—the people who sent the fake alert—access to his account. They stole thousands of confidential e-mails and documents.

More than 58,000 hacked messages from John Podesta's e-mail account were published.

PHASE 2

The hacked e-mails were released to the public by WikiLeaks, an international organization that publishes secret information. But that was not the only hack attack the Russian group made. A month later, computers at The Democratic Congressional Campaign Committee (DCCC) and the Democratic National Committee (DNC) were targeted. The hackers accessed the computer networks and installed malware to track user activity. It recorded anything that was typed. It also took screenshots of what was on the computer screens. Secret information such as passwords, banking details, and reports were stolen and released to the public at key times to harm the reputation of the party during the election campaign.

DARK SCIENCE SECRETS

WikiLeaks was formed in 2006 and describes itself as a not-for-profit media organization. That means WikiLeaks does not make money from the work it does. It has a website and a lot of secret contacts and information sources throughout the world. In 2010, WikiLeaks released hundreds of thousands of documents and files about the war in Afghanistan. The Afghan War documents leak revealed U.S. military secrets about the war. Many of them describe how civilians were killed. WikiLeaks has also released files on spies, torture, and where in the world wealthy people hide their money to avoid paying taxes.

DATA AND IDENTIFY THEFT

In 2013, actress Melissa McCarthy played a con artist in the comedy movie *Identity Thief*. In the movie, she steals the identity of a man named Sandy Patterson while he is buying identity theft protection. When he finds out that someone is pretending to be him and is using his credit card at a beauty salon, Patterson comes after his identity thief.

STEALING YOU

Unlike Sandy, most victims of identity theft do not know who is pretending to be them. Identity theft is one of the fastest-growing crimes. It happens when someone steals a person's personal information such as his or her name, address, social security or social insurance number, and e-mail address, and uses them without permission. Online identity thieves can be anywhere—in another city, state, province, or country. And they use a person's information for their own gain. In 2017, 15.4 million Americans were victims of some type of identity theft.

Actress Melissa McCarthy is shown here promoting her movie *Identity Thief*, at its premiere in Los Angeles.

IDENTITY HACKERS

People give their information to e-mail service providers, stores, and employers. Data breaches happen when the computer network of one of these places is hacked for information. A person's information can also be stolen if he or she provides it while using a public computer, or an **unsecured website**. An unsecured website is not **encrypted**, or coded. Many scammers use contests or offer free items to get people to provide their e-mail address and password. Scammers then use them to get more information about people.

Social Security numbers are given to each citizen in a country. They allow the person to work and to gain access to benefits. Identity thieves use them to get credit cards in another person's name.

DARK SCIENCE SECRETS

Denial of Service (DoS) attacks are cyberattacks that use data theft to disrupt a network, web, or Internet services to certain areas or companies. High-profile targets include hospitals and banks. The attacker tries to hold the target to ransom, either to get money or make a point. These attacks are becoming increasingly common. Each time they happen, we learn more about how to prevent them. Sometimes, victims know why they have been attacked and other times they have no clue. Occasionally, DoS attacks are training grounds for cyberattackers, so they can learn how their attack works best.

CYBER ESPIONAGE

Greg Walton was in the private office of the **Dalai Lama** in Dharamsala, India, in 2009 when he saw it. A computer "ghost" was stealing a copy of a confidential document right before his eyes. It was a major international crime, but there was nothing he could do to stop it. Later, in his lab in Toronto, Canada, he analyzed what had happened.

WHO IS STEALING OUR INFO?

As spiritual leader of the Tibetan people, the Dalai Lama and his representatives often meet with foreign leaders to press for Tibet's freedom. China claims Tibet as its own but the Dalai Lama and most Tibetans do not accept this. The Dalai Lama's office found that it would set up meetings with foreign leaders online, only to have information leaked and the meeting canceled. They thought someone was spying on them, and asked Greg Walton and others to investigate. Walton witnessed a theft, then investigated it.

Hackers stole more than a year's worth of the Dalai Lama's personal e-mails.

THE GHOSTNET

Back in Toronto, Walton and his Canadian team entered code from the Dalai Lama's infected computers into Google and discovered the **control servers** of a Chinese cyber spy network. The network, which they called GhostNet, had infected 1,200 computers around the world. GhostNet was a Chinese state-sponsored spying ring. Its purpose was to watch what Tibetans were doing. Monitoring Tibetans through a computer spying network is another way to control what Tibetans say and who they communicate with.

GhostNet is believed to have infected computers in 103 countries.

TOMORROW'S SECRETS

Botnets are networks of computers that act like zombies. They are sometimes even called zombie armies. The networks act in this way because they have been infected by a hacker's malware. The hacker can take control of thousands of computers and computer-connected devices to spread viruses and spam, steal data, and launch DoS attacks.

As hacker sophistication improves in the future, so too will botnet protections. Software companies constantly make new antivirus protection for computers to remove malicious files. But all computer experts warn that the first step in protection is to not download anything from unknown sources or click on links in e-mails from people you do not know. That way, hackers cannot gain access to home or business networks.

CHAPTER 4

PREDATORS AND PREY

More than 125 million people all over the world play the video game Fortnite Battle Royale. It is described by some experts as "a mass online brawl." The game is popular among young people aged 8 to 13. The game can be downloaded free of charge and played on almost any gaming platform. Because it is fun and free, Fortnite is great fun for kids who love computer games—but it also attracts cyber scammers.

TRICKING KIDS

In Fortnite, players can purchase in-game money called V-Bucks. Scammers target young players with fake offers for free V-bucks that show up on YouTube or other sites. When the link is clicked, malware is downloaded or players are asked for e-mail addresses and passwords. Some scammers sell cheap V-Bucks and ask children for their parents' credit card details.

Some games are exciting to play and can encourage kids to be reckless with their online information.

KID SAFETY

Cybercriminals know that kids love to play games such as Fortnite, so they offer free games and goods while stealing information. This is one of the many ways children are targeted online. The best ways to protect against these cyber predators are to use cybersecurity software and to never click on e-mails or texts from unknown people or on unknown websites. Above all, it is important to remember that if an offer sounds too good to be true, then it probably is.

DARK SCIENCE SECRETS

In 2017, more than 1 million children in the United States were the victims of online identity theft. Hackers target children because they have a smaller online history or record. In most cases, parents or children have no idea someone has stolen their information or is pretending to be them. Often, the information is grabbed by hackers in data breaches and is sold to people who create fake identities. They then apply for credit cards and use them to commit fraud. Sometimes, parents find out their children's identities have been stolen when they get a call from a **debt collector** who wants money from their child.

Young people are easy prey to online scammers because they are sometimes more trusting than adults.

CRIME SOURCING

Crowdsourcing is used to get a group of people to work toward a common goal. That goal may be quickly raising money for a cause, finding a solution to a problem, or getting a project done. In 2001, the computer company IBM started an online forum, called an Innovation Jam, to get the company's researchers and outside experts to find new ways of doing things. IBM used a bunch of different people, or "a crowd," to solve problems faster than IBM's researchers could do secretly in the lab.

CYBERCRIME SOURCING

Cybercriminals have adopted crowdsourcing to find new methods and targets for cybercrimes. Cybercriminals team up with organized crime groups, and know how to target computers and networks. Organized crime groups know how to extort money from people and companies. Together, they commit crimes online such as fraud, and find ways to hide the stolen money online.

Crowdsourcing can solve problems quickly because it uses the knowledge and skills of many different people at once.

GLOBAL BUSINESS

Crime sourcing is a global business. Criminal gangs contract, or give out, jobs to cybercriminals and hackers around the world. A cybercriminal in New York City may be working for an organized

crime gang in Tokyo. Cybercriminals specialize in different technical skills. Some write malware to infect computers and networks. Others rent and control botnets. Still others make sure the money made from cybercriminal enterprises is laundered. This means that the money is transferred into foreign banks or businesses to make it look legitimate—or at least not criminal.

DARK SCIENCE SECRETS

In 2010, the Infraud Organization was founded. It used an online forum to trade in stolen credit card and bank account numbers. "In fraud we trust" was their slogan, and stealing and selling U.S. social security numbers and bank account login information was their business. Their cheeky slogan was a play on the official "In God We Trust" motto of the United States. Police in the United States, Europe, Australia, and Asia worked together for years to find the cybercriminals. They believed there were 11,000 members.

In 2018, the U.S. Department of Justice **indicted**, or charged, 36 people for a number of crimes, including identity theft, fraud, and money laundering. However, only 13 of the criminals were found and arrested.

FRAUD ALERT

The Infraud Organization caused $530 million in losses to Americans.

LOST IN THE DARKNET

The **darknet** sounds like it is straight out of a science fiction novel. You cannot find it using Google, Bing, or Yahoo. But it is a hangout for people doing all sorts of shady cyber business, from buying and selling illegal goods, to finding criminals for hire. When a company or person's data is hacked and stolen, the darknet is where you will find it for sale.

Free speech activists in countries with little freedom of information say the darknet can help them spread information, such as where protests will be held.

NOT JUST CRIME

Of course, the darknet is not just for criminals. Some cyber experts use it for sharing confidential files. Activists use it for whistleblowing, or sharing information about wrongdoing. Some people use it for getting around Internet **censorship** rules and guidelines—they post things there that they cannot post on the regular Internet. All of these activities may or may not be against the law. An activist in a country with a violent and **oppressive** government might use the darknet to discuss how to fight back. They could not do this on the regular Internet without fear of imprisonment or death, because their comments would be monitored or their computer address identified.

LOCATION, LOCATION

Darknet surfers use The Online Router (Tor)—a free software program that sends messages through thousands of routes to conceal the users' location. Through Tor, users can surf the Internet and send messages **anonymously**, or without being identified. Tor can be used for good or bad purposes. The U.S. government helped develop Tor. The idea was to protect U.S. **intelligence communications**, or spying.

This is the webpage for Tor. It is a web browser that makes the user anonymous online.

DARK SCIENCE SECRETS

In 2016, researchers at King's College London, England, found that 57 percent of the sites designed for Tor are used for criminal activity. That criminal activity included dealing in illegal drugs, illegal money deals, and other wrongdoing. Researchers scanned 5,205 websites and found that 2,723 of them were doing shady business. Drugs and finance were the top uses, but terrorism, hacking, violence, and weapons dealing were also on the list.

FIGHTING CYBERCRIME

From police forces to secret services, spy agencies, and private cybersecurity, many agencies around the world fight cybercrime. Even white hat hackers help combat sinister cyber hacks. Policing the Internet and the darknet is time consuming and difficult.

Sony's hackers threatened terrorist attacks against movie theaters that played *The Interview.*

TRACKING A HACK

In 2014, Sony Pictures Entertainment was hacked. The FBI's intelligence agents tracked the hack to the North Korean government. During the hack, the company's internal data—all 38 million files—was stolen, made public, or sold. The files included movies that had not yet been released in theaters, and the personal information of people who worked at Sony. The movie company hired a cybersecurity company to track down the hackers. An FBI team also investigated.

OVER A MOVIE?

The investigators followed a number of trails. They used hacker tricks to figure out clues such as passwords or reused code. These clues were like digital fingerprints, which the investigators could trace back to the source of the hack. The hacker also made a threat against a movie Sony produced called *The Interview*. This led the FBI to believe the hackers were North Korean. *The Interview* is a comedy that features a ridiculous plot to kill North Korea's leader. In 2018, the U.S. Department of Justice pointed the finger at North Korea. It indicted one hacker. He was not the only hacker involved, but the secrecy of hacker networks and cybersecurity investigations make it difficult to identify others. North Korea has denied that the hacker even exists.

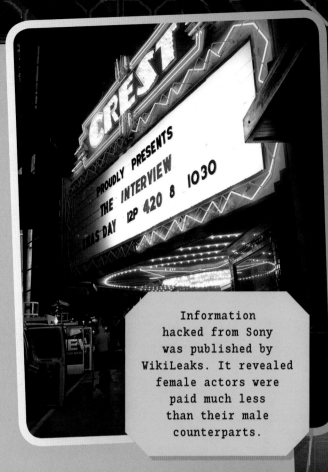

Information hacked from Sony was published by WikiLeaks. It revealed female actors were paid much less than their male counterparts.

TOMORROW'S SECRETS

The Internet Crime Complaint Center (IC3) is the FBI's "complaints central" for people who want to report Internet crime. If you are ever hacked, scammed, or taken advantage of, and want it known or investigated, you can report the incident to IC3 online or over the phone. IC3 also posts information on scams, and gives advice on how to protect your computer and personal information. Some of this advice includes routinely turning off and rebooting your computer. This small act temporarily disrupts malware used by cybercriminals. According to IC3, some cybercriminals use malware that can steal information or control your computer without you knowing it.

HACKERS GONE GOOD

A cybersecurity consultant is someone who advises companies and governments on how to keep their digital information safe and secure from hackers. When defending against the dark arts of cybercriminals, it can help to have insider knowledge. That is why some cybersecurity experts are former hackers who have left their criminal days behind for a job in the industries they used to target.

HACKERS NEEDED

Hackers are in demand for jobs at tech companies such as Google, Facebook, and Microsoft. Some companies even advertise for "ethical hackers." Ethical hackers are hired to try to break into company computer networks to find flaws in software. In other words, they think and work like a black hat hacker to help save the company from other black hats. White hat and ethical hacking has its appeal, but some hackers dabble in both black and white hacking.

WHITE HAT, DARK ART?

Marcus Hutchins is a British malware **analyst** who helped control the WannaCry cyberattack in the United Kingdom in 2016. Hutchins discovered a "kill switch" in WannaCry's code, and stopped it from spreading throughout the world—saving millions of computer networks and likely billions of dollars.

Hackers can use their skills to do good as well as bad. Doing bad usually pays more, but it carries a risk of a prison sentence.

Hero to some, Hutchins was considered an illegal hacker by the U.S. government. While attending the DEFCON hacker conference in Las Vegas, in 2017, he was arrested and charged with creating malware that collected bank account passwords. The malware was allegedly sold through a hidden site on the Tor network. Hutchins has pleaded not guilty to all the charges.

DEFCON held its first hacker conference in China in 2018.

TOMORROW'S SECRETS

Imagine that in the future, you become a hacker looking for a legal job in business or government. Where would you apply? You might try DEFCON, the world's largest hacker convention. DEFCON attendees include hackers as well as computer industry professionals, and law enforcement agents from the FBI and the Department of Defense (DoD). DEFCON hosts events and contests such as hacking competitions in which teams attack and defend computer networks. Black Hat is a computer security conference held just before DEFCON. Black Hat is thought to carry out hacking that occurs during the conference. Hackers have broken into hotel billing systems and hacked ATMs and the websites of other conference attendees.

FIGHTING SECRETS

Hacktivists are hackers who use their skills as instruments of **social change** or to promote a political opinion. Social change is progress in society as a result of behavioral and cultural changes. Many hacktivists have a strong belief in free speech and freedom of information. Some will break laws or act as whistleblowers to expose governments or businesses who they believe are not acting **ethically**, or morally right.

DIGITAL DISOBEDIENCE

When some people see wrongdoing, they use their freedom of expression to protest. In **democratic** countries, this is a human right. But when hacktivists see something wrong with the world, they hack for the cause. Hacktivism can be **disruptive**, with hackers breaking into websites

to change messages, or hacking private e-mails and making them public. They may even launch denial of service attacks to push a website offline for awhile.

ANONYMOUS ACTIONS

Anonymous is a hacktivist collective, or group. It has launched many campaigns and cyberattacks against

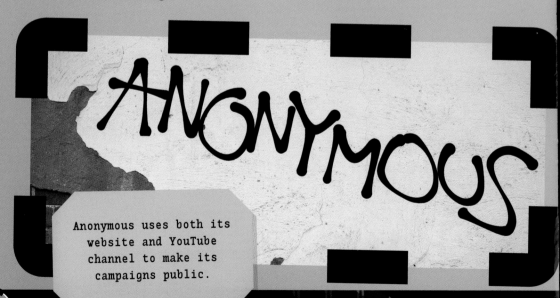

Anonymous uses both its website and YouTube channel to make its campaigns public.

governments and corporations that it sees as oppressive, corrupt, or not respectful of freedoms. Hackers work together on Anonymous attacks so they can remain unknown, and no single hacker takes credit.

Anonymous has launched cyberattacks on terrorist group Islamic State (IS), raised awareness of homelessness, and protested the shootings of unarmed African-American men.

TOMORROW'S SECRETS

Protestors show support for Edward Snowden at a rally. Some people consider him a traitor for sharing secrets, while others think he shone a light on unfair practices.

STOP MASS SPYING

We the People
Oppose the Surveillance State and say:

THANK YOU, EDWARD SNOWDEN!

TAKE ACTION AT
Than   Snowden.o
Partn   rit

STOP MASS SPYING
stopwatching.us

In 2013, Edward Snowden made the biggest leak of secret documents in U.S. history. He worked for the National Security Administration (NSA), a government organization. Snowden found that the government was spying on its citizens by gathering information from Facebook, Google, and Microsoft. Snowden leaked top secret documents on government surveillance to newspapers, and exposed cyber warfare programs being developed by governments. He fled to Russia after the U.S. government charged him with theft of government property and espionage. He still lives in Russia.

A new law now means the NSA cannot collect information in bulk, as it had been doing before Snowden's leak. Snowden's leaks have also paved the way for the first ever data privacy bill of **rights** in the near future. It will require social media companies to notify users of a breach.

WHAT NEXT?

Hackers know that most people in the world are not truly aware of the dangers of cyber warfare. Cyber warfare is the computer-based attack on one country by another. Hackers are the army, and computer code is the weaponry. Our increasing reliance on computers means that we are vulnerable to this kind of warfare.

The stock market, where traders buy and sell shares of businesses, is an ideal cyber warfare target because many people would lose money in an attack. This would cause chaos and instability.

A DIFFERENT KIND OF WAR

The main targets of a cyber war will be **infrastructure**, which is the physical structures and services that are needed for a country to operate. These include power supplies and public utilities such as nuclear power plants and water supplies, and also banking systems, hospital computer systems, and schools. Many of the computer systems that run these utilities and services were built in the 1980s and 1990s when cybersecurity was less of a concern—meaning they have fewer defenses. By messing with the flow of goods and services, cyber terrorists can inflict heavy financial damage.

DARK SCIENCE SECRETS

Cyberterrorism is described as the use of the Internet to carry out violent or harmful acts. It is often done to achieve a political goal. Cyberterrorism also includes helping known terrorist groups achieve their aims. In 2016, a hacker was sentenced to 20 years in jail. He had stolen personal information about U.S. government and military workers to help IS. He was the first hacker prosecuted on terrorism charges in the United States. The 20-year-old from Kosovo in eastern Europe gave more than 1,000 names to IS with the understanding that it would conduct terrorist attacks against these people.

ALREADY HAPPENING

In 2013, hackers attacked a small dam in Rye Brook, New York, 25 miles (40 km) north of New York City. The cyberattackers used a **cellular modem** to take control of the dam's operating system. The aim was to force the gate open and cause a flood to destroy infrastructure. Fortunately, the hack did no damage but only because a gate had been disconnected for maintenance at the time. The hackers were located in Iran. The **intrusion** happened when the United States and Iran were negotiating a deal on limiting Iran's nuclear program. Experts believe it was a warning to the United States about Iran's ability to harm U.S. infrastructure through cyber warfare.

In 2018, an airport in Bristol, England, suffered a ransomware attack. The hackers wanted to cause chaos with delayed flights so they could extort money from the airport or airlines and show how powerful they were.

THE FUTURE OF CYBERCRIME

Cybersecurity experts see two new trends that will change the face of cybercrime and cybersecurity. They both involve computer systems doing much of the work now done by all kinds of hackers. **Artificial intelligence (AI)** and **machine learning** are giving computer systems the ability to learn without being programmed.

PREDICTING CYBER MONEY LAUNDERING

With cybercrime costing banks and businesses around $600 billion a year, machine learning will more accurately detect banking irregularities from hacking. Each year, up to $200 billion in cybercrime proceeds is laundered throughout the globe. Machine learning processes are more accurate at making sense of data than regular computer programming because the computer learns to recognize patterns.

Lost and stolen money and identities, and cybercrime protection, come at a high cost.

ADAPTIVE MALWARE

Industry experts believe **adaptive malware**, or malware that uses artificial intelligence, is coming our way very soon. Knowing about the potential threats and where they are coming from is called "threat intelligence." Computer companies such as Microsoft have developed threat intelligence tools that gather information from services and networks, including e-mails and the Internet Explorer web browser, to watch for signs of threats.

TOMORROW'S SECRETS

Hacktivists fear that the ongoing threat of cybercrime will force governments to pass stronger national security laws. These laws will aim to protect, but they may also endanger personal privacy and security. Hacktivists also fear an increased cyber **arms race** in which different countries and their hacker armies use cyberattacks on citizens to achieve political gains. These attacks might be used to pull back on freedoms. Some hacktivist groups are launching their own cyberattacks in protest of these laws and government actions. Some groups have targeted cities and smaller governments already. Cybersecurity experts worry hacktivists are getting more extreme in their thinking.

BE A CYBERCRIME SPECIALIST

We have seen how the Internet and darknet have been used for crimes against individuals, organizations, and countries. Imagine you are a cybercrime specialist and your mission is to learn about the most threatening cybercrimes—and develop a plan to fight them.

YOUR MISSION

- Research which aspects of cybercrime you think are most threatening. Which would you like to fight, if you were a cybercrime specialist? For example, are you interested in protecting people's identities through laws or through cybersecurity practices? Or maybe you are interested in understanding computer code, so that you can become a white hat hacker? Learn about what these people do.

- Research what you would need to develop a cybersecurity system. What kind of experience and education would you need to join a cybersecurity team?

- What have you learned from this book that could help you? Have you learned that understanding computers and computer networks requires a certain skill set? What other skills would help you combat cybercrime?

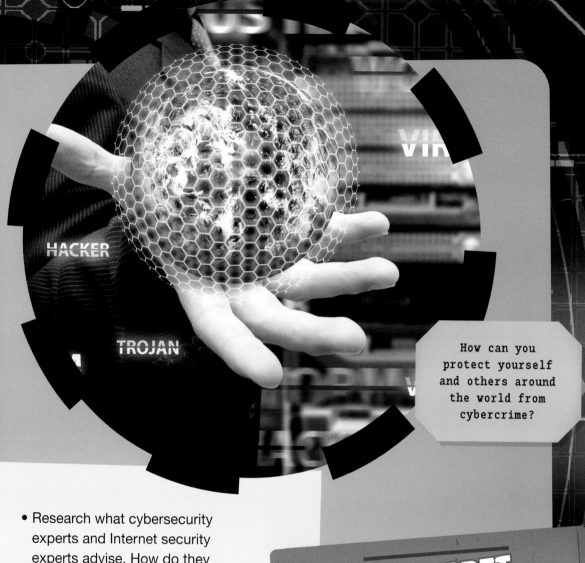

HACKER

TROJAN

VIR

How can you
protect yourself
and others around
the world from
cybercrime?

- Research what cybersecurity
  experts and Internet security
  experts advise. How do they
  improve their technical and
  critical thinking skills?

- Compile what you have learned
  into a report that details the threat
  being faced, the team that will be
  required, and the plan of action
  you and the team will take to fight
  the cybercrime. What would your
  cybersecurity system look like?

TOP SECRET

Would you sell your protection
plans, or would you share your
knowledge with the world, so that
everybody knew about it? Do you
think completed cybersecurity
systems should be kept secret?
Explain your decision.

45

GLOSSARY

Please note: Some **bold-faced** words are defined where they appear in the book.

agency A government organization that provides a service

analyst A person who studies the operations or data and information processing of a computer

arms race An unofficial competition between countries to have a superior number of military arms

artificial intelligence (AI) The ability of a computer to perform tasks that usually require human intelligence, such as learning and reasoning

breach The release or theft of secure or private information by an unauthorized individual or group

cellular modem A device that allows wireless connection to the Internet

censorship Examining what people do on computers for the purpose of preventing them from doing it

coding The computer language used to develop software and websites

confidence schemes Scams that involve gaining a person's trust, then stealing from them

control servers A computer commanded and controlled by a cyber attacker or cybercriminal, which is used to send commands to computers and networks controlled by malware

cybercriminals People who commit crimes on computers and the Internet

cyberstalker Someone that relentlessly pursues their victim online

Dalai Lama The spiritual leader and chief monk of Tibet

debt collector A company that works on behalf of another to try to get people to pay money owed to that company

democratic A form of government in which people choose leaders by voting

digital rights The rights that allow a person to access, create, and use content on the Internet without it being censored or stolen

disruptive Causing disorder

economic Related to money and business

e-mail service providers Companies that offer e-mail accounts to their customers

espionage Spying by a government to discover the political and military secrets of other nations

fraud Deceit or misleading lies used for profit or in a crime

hackers People who break into computer programs

identity Personal information such as name, birth date, and address

incursions Invasions or raids

indicted Charged with a crime

Interpol An international police agency of 100 countries

intrusion Entering and taking possession of property, or data on a computer

laundering money Taking money earned through crime and making it look as though it was earned legitimately

machine learning Describes the way that computers learn to identify patterns in data and make decisions without human input

malicious With ill intent

malware Software that damages a computer

networks Groups that share information

nuclear To do with the production of nuclear materials, weapons, or power

online forums Internet message boards where people can hold discussions

operative A spy or secret agent

oppressive Harsh and controlling

programmers People skilled in writing computer code

ransomware Malicious software designed to hold the user ransom

rights Things that people are morally or legally entitled to have

security consultant A person paid to keep computer systems safe and private

software Programs used by computers

terrorism Use of violence to achieve a goal

trade secrets Secret methods used by a company to make products

video streaming devices Devices that connect a television to the Internet and allow a person to see movies from online sources

LEARNING MORE

BOOKS

Higgins, Melissa, and Michael Regan. *Cybersecurity* (Special Reports). ABDO Publishing Company, 2015.

Hyde, Natalie. *Net Neutrality* (Get Informed, Stay Informed). Crabtree Publishing, 2018.

Hynson, Colin. *Cyber Crime* (Inside Crime). Smart Apple Media, 2011.

Mara, Wil. *Cybercriminals* (True Books). Scholastic, 2016.

WEBSITES

http://mediasmarts.ca/sites/mediasmarts/files/games/privacy_playground/flash/privacy_playground_en/start.html
   Play The First Adventure of the Three CyberPigs game to learn all about privacy online.

https://sos.fbi.gov
   Try out the FBI's cybersafety game site to learn more about keeping safe online.

www.att.com/Common/images/safety/game.html
   Play the AT&T Safety Land Game to learn how to keep safe from cybercrime.

www.blue-pencil.ca/top-12-cyber-crime-facts-and-statistics
   Visit this site for facts and statistics on cybercrime.

INDEX

ABOUT THE AUTHOR

Ellen Rodger is a writer and editor who has written about fleas, hurricanes, potatoes, sewer systems, and solar systems. She enjoys hiking, reading, and hearing people tell their stories.